MDCOUC

GOD'S BLESSINGS FOR

MOTHERS

COMPILED BY

JACK COUNTRYMAN

COUNTRYMAN

A Division of Thomas Nelson Publishers

THOMAS NELSON
Since 1798

NASHVILLE DALLAS MEXICO CITY RIO DE JANEIRO

Published in Nashville, Tennessee, by Thomas
Nelson. Thomas Nelson is a trademark of
Thomas Nelson, Inc.

Thomas Nelson, Inc., titles may be purchased in
bulk for educational, business, fund-raising, or
sales promotional use. For information, please
e-mail SpecialMarkets@ThomasNelson.com.

ISBN-13: 978-1-4003-2183-4 (display)
ISBN-13: 978-1-4003-2184-1

Printed in the United States of America

13 14 15 16 17 PP 5 4 3 2 1

www.thomasnelson.com

TABLE OF CONTENTS

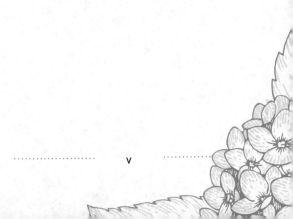

INTRODUCTION

*"Her children rise up
and call her blessed."*

Proverbs 31:28

*G*od desires to bless those mothers who long for Him as their loving, caring heavenly Father. Through Scripture, He has designed a pathway to encourage you in your role of motherhood. We hope that this book will give you a sense of purpose and meaning as you experience *God's Blessings for Mothers.*

For I know the thoughts that I think toward you, says the LORD, thoughts of peace and not of evil, to give you a future and a hope. Then you will call upon Me and go and pray to Me, and I will listen to you. And you will seek Me and find Me, when you search for Me with all your heart.

Jeremiah 29:11–13

God Blesses
Mothers Who
Are ...

Confident in Him

In You, O Lord, I put my trust;
 Let me never be put to shame.
Deliver me in Your righteousness, and
  cause me to escape;
  Incline Your ear to me, and save
  me. . . .
For You are my hope, O Lord God;
 You are my trust from my youth.

Psalm 71:1–2, 5

The Lord shall preserve you from all evil;
 He shall preserve your soul.
The Lord shall preserve your going out
  and your coming in
  From this time forth, and even
  forevermore.

Psalm 121:7–8

It is better to trust in the LORD
> Than to put confidence in man.

Psalm 118:8

For the LORD will be your confidence,
> And will keep your foot from being
> caught.

Proverbs 3:26

But the Lord is faithful, who will establish you and guard you from the evil one. And we have confidence in the Lord concerning you, both that you do and will do the things we command you.

2 Thessalonians 3:3–4

Now this is the confidence that we have in Him, that if we ask anything according to His will, He hears us. And if we know that He hears us, whatever we ask, we know that we have the petitions that we have asked of Him.

1 John 5:14–15

Growing in Him

"You did not choose Me, but I chose you and appointed you that you should go and bear fruit, and that your fruit should remain, that whatever you ask the Father in My name He may give you."

John 15:16

But to you who fear My name
  The Sun of Righteousness shall arise
  With healing in His wings;
  And you shall go out
  And grow fat like stall-fed calves.

Malachi 4:2

I will instruct you and teach you in the
    way you should go;
  I will guide you with My eye.

Psalm 32:8

So I have looked for You in the
　　sanctuary,
　　To see Your power and Your glory.
Because Your lovingkindness is better
　　than life,
　　My lips shall praise You.
Thus I will bless You while I live;
　　I will lift up my hands in Your
　　　name. . . .
Because You have been my help,
　　Therefore in the shadow of Your
　　　wings I will rejoice.

Psalm 63:2–4, 7

Speaking the truth in love, [we] may grow up in all things into Him who is the head—Christ—from whom the whole body, joined and knit together by what every joint supplies, according to the effective working by which every part does its share, causes growth of the body for the edifying of itself in love.

Ephesians 4:15–16

Serving Him

"If anyone serves Me, let him follow Me; and where I am, there My servant will be also. If anyone serves Me, him My Father will honor."

John 12:26

Command those who are rich in this present age not to be haughty, nor to trust in uncertain riches but in the living God, who gives us richly all things to enjoy. Let them do good, that they be rich in good works, ready to give, willing to share, storing up for themselves a good foundation for the time to come, that they may lay hold on eternal life.

1 Timothy 6:17–19

But let each one examine his own work, and then he will have rejoicing in himself alone, and not in another. For each one shall bear his own load.

Let him who is taught the word share in all good things with him who teaches. . . .

And let us not grow weary while doing good, for in due season we shall reap if we do not lose heart.

Galatians 6:4–6, 9

Now therefore, fear the LORD, serve Him in sincerity and in truth, and put away the gods which your fathers served on the other side of the River and in Egypt. Serve the LORD! And if it seems evil to you to serve the LORD, choose for yourselves this day whom you will serve, whether the gods which your fathers served that were on the other side of the River, or the gods of the Amorites, in whose land you dwell. But as for me and my house, we will serve the LORD.

Joshua 24:14–15

Serve the LORD with gladness;
Come before His presence with
singing.
Know that the LORD, He is God;
It is He who has made us, and not
we ourselves;
We are His people and the sheep of
His pasture.

Psalm 100:2–3

"By this all will know that you are My disciples, if you have love for one another."

John 13:35

Seeking Him

O God, You are my God;
  Early will I seek You;
  My soul thirsts for You;
  My flesh longs for You
  In a dry and thirsty land
  Where there is no water.

Psalm 63:1

"I love those who love me,
  And those who seek me diligently
    will find me."

Proverbs 8:17

I sought the Lᴏʀᴅ, and He heard me,
  And delivered me from all my fears.

Psalm 34:4

Seek the Lord and His strength;
 Seek His face evermore!
Remember His marvelous works which
  He has done,
  His wonders, and the judgments of
  His mouth.

1 Chronicles 16:11–12

Seek the Lord while He may be found,
 Call upon Him while He is near.

Isaiah 55:6

The young lions lack and suffer hunger;
 But those who seek the Lord shall
  not lack any good thing.

Psalm 34:10

"Ask, and it will be given to you; seek, and you will find; knock, and it will be opened to you. For everyone who asks receives, and he who seeks finds, and to him who knocks it will be opened."

Matthew 7:7–8

Showing Him to Others

So then, my beloved brethren, let every man be swift to hear, slow to speak, slow to wrath; for the wrath of man does not produce the righteousness of God.

Therefore lay aside all filthiness and overflow of wickedness, and receive with meekness the implanted word, which is able to save your souls. . . .

Pure and undefiled religion before God and the Father is this: to visit orphans and widows in their trouble, and to keep oneself unspotted from the world.

James 1:19–21, 27

Will You not revive us again,

That Your people may rejoice in You?
Show us Your mercy, LORD,

And grant us Your salvation.

Psalm 85:6–7

Now by this we know that we know Him, if we keep His commandments. He who says, "I know Him," and does not keep His commandments, is a liar, and the truth is not in him. But whoever keeps His word, truly the love of God is perfected in him. By this we know that we are in Him.

1 John 2:3–5

But someone will say, "You have faith, and I have works." Show me your faith without your works, and I will show you my faith by my works. You believe that there is one God. You do well. Even the demons believe—and tremble! But do you want to know, O foolish man, that faith without works is dead? Was not Abraham our father justified by works when he offered Isaac his son on the altar? Do you see that faith was working together with his works, and by works faith was made perfect?

James 2:18–22

Therefore, having been justified by faith, we have peace with God through our Lord Jesus Christ, through whom also we have access by faith into this grace in which we stand, and rejoice in hope of the glory of God. And not only that, but we also glory in tribulations, knowing that tribulation produces perseverance; and perseverance, character; and character, hope.

Romans 5:1–4

"Thus says the LORD of hosts:
'Execute true justice,
Show mercy and compassion
Everyone to his brother.
Do not oppress the widow or the
fatherless,
The alien or the poor.
Let none of you plan evil in his
heart
Against his brother.'"

Zechariah 7:9–10

Obeying Him

"If you love Me, keep My commandments."

John 14:15

"Whoever comes to Me, and hears My sayings and does them, I will show you whom he is like: He is like a man building a house, who dug deep and laid the foundation on the rock. And when the flood arose, the stream beat vehemently against that house, and could not shake it, for it was founded on the rock. But he who heard and did nothing is like a man who built a house on the earth without a foundation, against which the stream beat vehemently; and immediately it fell. And the ruin of that house was great."

Luke 6:47–49

"But this is what I commanded them, saying, 'Obey My voice, and I will be your God, and you shall be My people. And walk in all the ways that I have commanded you, that it may be well with you.'"

Jeremiah 7:23

"Even those from afar shall come and build the temple of the Lord. Then you shall know that the Lord of hosts has sent Me to you. And this shall come to pass if you diligently obey the voice of the Lord your God."

Zechariah 6:15

And having been perfected, He became the author of eternal salvation to all who obey Him.

Hebrews 5:9

Focusing on His Love

But whoever has this world's goods, and sees his brother in need, and shuts up his heart from him, how does the love of God abide in him?

My little children, let us not love in word or in tongue, but in deed and in truth. And by this we know that we are of the truth, and shall assure our hearts before Him.

1 John 3:17–19

For I am persuaded that neither death nor life, nor angels nor principalities nor powers, nor things present nor things to come, nor height nor depth, nor any other created thing, shall be able to separate us from the love of God which is in Christ Jesus our Lord.

Romans 8:38–39

For God has not given us a spirit of fear, but of power and of love and of a sound mind.

Therefore do not be ashamed of the testimony of our Lord, nor of me His prisoner, but share with me in the sufferings for the gospel according to the power of God, who has saved us and called us with a holy calling, not according to our works, but according to His own purpose and grace which was given to us in Christ Jesus before time began.

2 Timothy 1:7–9

"Teacher, which is the great commandment in the law?"

Jesus said to him, " 'You shall love the LORD your God with all your heart, with all your soul, and with all your mind.' This is the first and great commandment. And the second is like it: 'You shall love your neighbor as yourself.' "

Matthew 22:36–39

In this the love of God was manifested toward us, that God has sent His only begotten Son into the world, that we might live through Him. In this is love, not that we loved God, but that He loved us and sent His Son to be the propitiation for our sins. Beloved, if God so loved us, we also ought to love one another.

1 John 4:9–11

For this is the love of God, that we keep His commandments. And His commandments are not burdensome. For whatever is born of God overcomes the world. And this is the victory that has overcome the world—our faith. Who is he who overcomes the world, but he who believes that Jesus is the Son of God?

1 John 5:3–5

Choosing to Be His Friend

"This is My commandment, that you love one another as I have loved you. Greater love has no one than this, than to lay down one's life for his friends. You are My friends if you do whatever I command you. No longer do I call you servants, for a servant does not know what his master is doing; but I have called you friends, for all things that I heard from My Father I have made known to you."

John 15:12–15

Let brotherly love continue. Do not forget to entertain strangers, for by so doing some have unwittingly entertained angels.

Hebrews 13:1–2

He who covers a transgression seeks
    love,
    But he who repeats a matter
      separates friends.

Proverbs 17:9

A friend loves at all times,
    And a brother is born for adversity.

Proverbs 17:17

A man who has friends must himself be
    friendly,
    But there is a friend who sticks
      closer than a brother.

Proverbs 18:24

Do not forsake your own friend or your
    father's friend,
    Nor go to your brother's house in
      the day of your calamity;
    Better is a neighbor nearby than a
      brother far away.

Proverbs 27:10

GOD BLESSES MOTHERS WHO ARE...
Worshiping Him

Give unto the LORD, O you mighty ones,
  Give unto the LORD glory and
    strength.
Give unto the LORD the glory due to His
  name;
  Worship the LORD in the beauty of
    holiness.

Psalm 29:1–2

Oh come, let us worship and bow down;
  Let us kneel before the LORD our
    Maker.
For He is our God,
  And we are the people of His
    pasture,
  And the sheep of His hand.

Psalm 95:6–7

"Then you will call upon Me and go and pray to Me, and I will listen to you. And you will seek Me and find Me, when you search for Me with all your heart."

Jeremiah 29:12–13

Seek the LORD and His strength;
    Seek His face evermore!
Remember His marvelous works which
        He has done,
        His wonders, and the judgments of
        His mouth!

1 Chronicles 16:11–12

Give to the LORD the glory due His
        name;
    Bring an offering, and come before
        Him.
    Oh, worship the LORD in the beauty
        of holiness!

1 Chronicles 16:29

Coming to Him in Prayer

Give ear, O Lᴏʀᴅ, to my prayer;
  And attend to the voice of my
    supplications.
In the day of my trouble I will call upon
      You,
    For You will answer me.

Psalm 86:6–7

"And when you pray, you shall not be like the hypocrites. For they love to pray standing in the synagogues and on the corners of the streets, that they may be seen by men. Assuredly, I say to you, they have their reward. But you, when you pray, go into your room, and when you have shut your door, pray to your Father who is in the secret place; and your Father who sees in secret will reward you openly."

Matthew 6:5–6

You will make your prayer to Him,
   He will hear you,
   And you will pay your vows.
You will also declare a thing,
   And it will be established for you;
   So light will shine on your ways.

Job 22:27–28

"Call to Me, and I will answer you, and show you great and mighty things, which you do not know."

Jeremiah 33:3

Pray without ceasing, in everything give thanks; for this is the will of God in Christ Jesus for you.

1 Thessalonians 5:17–18

Let us therefore come boldly to the throne of grace, that we may obtain mercy and find grace to help in time of need.

Hebrews 4:16

Listening to the Holy Spirit

"But the Helper, the Holy Spirit, whom the Father will send in My name, He will teach you all things, and bring to your remembrance all things that I said to you."

John 14:26

"However, when He, the Spirit of truth, has come, He will guide you into all truth; for He will not speak on His own authority, but whatever He hears He will speak; and He will tell you things to come."

John 16:13

"For the Holy Spirit will teach you in that very hour what you ought to say."

Luke 12:12

For what man knows the things of a man except the spirit of the man which is in him? Even so no one knows the things of God except the Spirit of God. Now we have received, not the spirit of the world, but the Spirit who is from God, that we might know the things that have been freely given to us by God.

These things we also speak, not in words which man's wisdom teaches but which the Holy Spirit teaches, comparing spiritual things with spiritual.

1 Corinthians 2:11–13

Not by works of righteousness which we have done, but according to His mercy He saved us, through the washing of regeneration and renewing of the Holy Spirit, whom He poured out on us abundantly through Jesus Christ our Savior.

Titus 3:5–6

But if the Spirit of Him who raised Jesus from the dead dwells in you, He who raised Christ from the dead will also give life to your mortal bodies through His Spirit who dwells in you. . . .

The Spirit Himself bears witness with our spirit that we are children of God, and if children, then heirs—heirs of God and joint heirs with Christ, if indeed we suffer with Him, that we may also be glorified together.

For I consider that the sufferings of this present time are not worthy to be compared with the glory which shall be revealed in us. . . .

Likewise the Spirit also helps in our weaknesses. For we do not know what we should pray for as we ought, but the Spirit Himself makes intercession for us with groanings which cannot be uttered.

Romans 8:11, 16–18, 26

God

Encourages

Mothers to . . .

Give to Others with Grace

He has shown you, O man, what is
    good;
    And what does the Lord require of
      you
    But to do justly,
    To love mercy,
    And to walk humbly with your
      God?

Micah 6:8

"Give, and it will be given to you: good measure, pressed down, shaken together, and running over will be put into your bosom. For with the same measure that you use, it will be measured back to you."

Luke 6:38

By this we know love, because He laid down His life for us. And we also ought to lay down our lives for the brethren. But whoever has this world's goods, and sees his brother in need, and shuts up his heart from him, how does the love of God abide in him?

1 John 3:16–17

Not returning evil for evil or reviling for reviling, but on the contrary blessing, knowing that you were called to this, that you may inherit a blessing.

1 Peter 3:9

And let us not grow weary while doing good, for in due season we shall reap if we do not lose heart.

Galatians 6:9

Jesus said to him, "If you want to be perfect, go, sell what you have and give to the poor, and you will have treasure in heaven; and come, follow Me."

Matthew 19:21

Live Lives of Service

"A new commandment I give to you, that you love one another; as I have loved you, that you also love one another. By this all will know that you are My disciples, if you have love for one another."

John 13:34–35

As each one has received a gift, minister it to one another, as good stewards of the manifold grace of God. If anyone speaks, let him speak as the oracles of God. If anyone ministers, let him do it as with the ability which God supplies, that in all things God may be glorified through Jesus Christ, to whom belong the glory and the dominion forever and ever. Amen.

1 Peter 4:10–11

"And whoever desires to be first among you, let him be your slave—just as the Son of Man did not come to be served, but to serve, and to give His life a ransom for many."

Matthew 20:27–28

And whatever you do, do it heartily, as to the Lord and not to men, knowing that from the Lord you will receive the reward of the inheritance; for you serve the Lord Christ. But he who does wrong will be repaid for what he has done, and there is no partiality.

Colossians 3:23–25

For you, brethren, have been called to liberty; only do not use liberty as an opportunity for the flesh, but through love serve one another. For all the law is fulfilled in one word, even in this: "You shall love your neighbor as yourself."

Galatians 5:13–14

Offer Encouragement to Others

Therefore comfort each other and edify one another, just as you also are doing.

1 Thessalonians 5:11

Therefore let us pursue the things which make for peace and the things by which one may edify another.

Romans 14:19

And let us consider one another in order to stir up love and good works, not forsaking the assembling of ourselves together, as is the manner of some, but exhorting one another, and so much the more as you see the Day approaching.

Hebrews 10:24–25

But if we walk in the light as He is in the light, we have fellowship with one another, and the blood of Jesus Christ His Son cleanses us from all sin.

1 John 1:7

Brethren, if a man is overtaken in any trespass, you who are spiritual restore such a one in a spirit of gentleness, considering yourself lest you also be tempted. Bear one another's burdens, and so fulfill the law of Christ.

Galatians 6:1–2

And be kind to one another, tender-hearted, forgiving one another, even as God in Christ forgave you.

Therefore be imitators of God as dear children. And walk in love, as Christ also has loved us and given Himself for us, an offering and a sacrifice to God for a sweet-smelling aroma.

Ephesians 4:32–5:2

Pray for One Another

"For the eyes of the LORD are on the
righteous,
And His ears are open to their
prayers;
But the face of the LORD is against
those who do evil."
And who is he who will harm you if
you become followers of what is good?

1 Peter 3:12–13

And take the helmet of salvation, and the
sword of the Spirit, which is the word of
God; praying always with all prayer and
supplication in the Spirit, being watchful to this end with all perseverance and
supplication for all the saints.

Ephesians 6:17–18

Now this is the confidence that we have in Him, that if we ask anything according to His will, He hears us. And if we know that He hears us, whatever we ask, we know that we have the petitions that we have asked of Him.

1 John 5:14–15

Give heed to the voice of my cry,
    My King and my God,
    For to You I will pray.
My voice You shall hear in the morning,
      O LORD;
    In the morning I will direct it to
      You,
    And I will look up.

Psalm 5:2–3

Rejoice always, pray without ceasing, in everything give thanks; for this is the will of God in Christ Jesus for you.

1 Thessalonians 5:16–18

Cherish Their Families

"This is My commandment, that you love one another as I have loved you."

John 15:12

Our presentable parts have no need. But God composed the body, having given greater honor to that part which lacks it, that there should be no schism in the body, but that the members should have the same care for one another. And if one member suffers, all the members suffer with it; or if one member is honored, all the members rejoice with it.

1 Corinthians 12:24–26

God sets the solitary in families;
    He brings out those who are bound
        into prosperity;
    But the rebellious dwell in a dry land.

Psalm 68:6

Two are better than one,
    Because they have a good reward for
        their labor.
For if they fall, one will lift up his
        companion.
    But woe to him who is alone when
        he falls,
    For he has no one to help him up.
Again, if two lie down together, they
        will keep warm;
    But how can one be warm alone?

Ecclesiastes 4:9–11

Watch, stand fast in the faith, be brave, be strong. Let all that you do be done with love.

1 Corinthians 16:13–14

Celebrate God's Love with Joy

I will sing of the mercies of the LORD
    forever;
    With my mouth will I make
        known Your faithfulness to all
        generations.

Psalm 89:1

I will meditate on Your precepts,
    And contemplate Your ways.
I will delight myself in Your statutes;
    I will not forget Your word.
Deal bountifully with Your servant,
    That I may live and keep Your word.

Psalm 119:15–17

And it will be said in that day:
"Behold, this is our God;
We have waited for Him, and He
will save us.
This is the Lord;
We have waited for Him;
We will be glad and rejoice in His
salvation."

Isaiah 25:9

"The Lord your God in your midst,
The Mighty One, will save;
He will rejoice over you with
gladness,
He will quiet you with His love,
He will rejoice over you with
singing."

Zephaniah 3:17

Jesus said to him, "You shall love the Lord your God with all your heart, with all your soul, and with all your mind."

Matthew 22:37

Rejoice in the Lord always. Again I will say, rejoice!

Let your gentleness be known to all men. The Lord is at hand.

Philippians 4:4–5

Now hope does not disappoint, because the love of God has been poured out in our hearts by the Holy Spirit who was given to us.

Romans 5:5

God Comforts

Mothers as They

Learn to ...

Handle Spiritual Trials

But, beloved, do not forget this one thing, that with the Lord one day is as a thousand years, and a thousand years as one day. The Lord is not slack concerning His promise, as some count slackness, but is longsuffering toward us, not willing that any should perish but that all should come to repentance.

2 Peter 3:8–9

Yet if anyone suffers as a Christian, let him not be ashamed, but let him glorify God in this matter.

1 Peter 4:16

He who covers his sins will not prosper,
But whoever confesses and forsakes
them will have mercy.

Proverbs 28:13

Blessed are those who keep His
      testimonies,
  Who seek Him with the whole heart!

Psalm 119:2

Beloved, do not think it strange concerning the fiery trial which is to try you, as though some strange thing happened to you; but rejoice to the extent that you partake of Christ's sufferings, that when His glory is revealed, you may also be glad with exceeding joy.

1 Peter 4:12–13

Hear me, O LORD, for Your
      lovingkindness is good;
  Turn to me according to the
      multitude of Your tender mercies.
And do not hide Your face from Your
      servant,
  For I am in trouble;
  Hear me speedily.
Draw near to my soul, and redeem it;
  Deliver me because of my enemies.

Psalm 69:16–18

Confront Serious Illness

Heal me, O LORD, and I shall be healed;
Save me, and I shall be saved,
For You are my praise.

Jeremiah 17:14

Blessed be the God and Father of our
Lord Jesus Christ, the Father of mercies
and God of all comfort, who comforts us
in all our tribulation, that we may be able
to comfort those who are in any trouble,
with the comfort with which we ourselves are comforted by God.

2 Corinthians 1:3–4

For this is God,
Our God forever and ever;
He will be our guide
Even to death.

Psalm 48:14

Who shall separate us from the love of Christ? Shall tribulation, or distress, or persecution, or famine, or nakedness, or peril, or sword? . . .

Yet in all these things we are more than conquerors through Him who loved us. For I am persuaded that neither death nor life, nor angels nor principalities nor powers, nor things present nor things to come, nor height nor depth, nor any other created thing, shall be able to separate us from the love of God which is in Christ Jesus our Lord.

Romans 8:35, 37–39

Yea, though I walk through the valley
    of the shadow of death,
    I will fear no evil;
    For You are with me;
    Your rod and Your staff, they
        comfort me.

Psalm 23:4

Deal with Financial Stress

And the Lord said, "Who then is that faithful and wise steward, whom his master will make ruler over his household, to give them their portion of food in due season? Blessed is that servant whom his master will find so doing when he comes. Truly, I say to you that he will make him ruler over all that he has."

Luke 12:42–44

And my God shall supply all your need according to His riches in glory by Christ Jesus.

Philippians 4:19

Listen, my beloved brethren: Has God not chosen the poor of this world to be rich in faith and heirs of the kingdom which He promised to those who love Him?

James 2:5

Then He said to His disciples, "Therefore I say to you, do not worry about your life, what you will eat; nor about the body, what you will put on. Life is more than food, and the body is more than clothing. Consider the ravens, for they neither sow nor reap, which have neither storehouse nor barn; and God feeds them. Of how much more value are you than the birds?"

Luke 12:22–24

In the house of the righteous there is
    much treasure,
  But in the revenue of the wicked is
    trouble.

Proverbs 15:6

Be anxious for nothing, but in everything by prayer and supplication, with thanksgiving, let your requests be made known to God; and the peace of God, which surpasses all understanding, will guard your hearts and minds through Christ Jesus.

Philippians 4:6–7

"Lay up for yourselves treasures in heaven, where neither moth nor rust destroys and where thieves do not break in and steal. For where your treasure is, there your heart will be also."

Matthew 6:20–21

Face the Years Ahead

The righteous shall flourish like a palm
tree,
He shall grow like a cedar in
Lebanon.
Those who are planted in the house of
the LORD
Shall flourish in the courts of our
God.
They shall still bear fruit in old age;
They shall be fresh and flourishing,
To declare that the LORD is upright;
He is my rock, and there is no
unrighteousness in Him.

Psalm 92:12–15

For I know that my Redeemer lives,
  And He shall stand at last on the
    earth;
And after my skin is destroyed, this I
  know,
    That in my flesh I shall see God.

Job 19:25–26

But as for me, I trust in You, O Lord;
  I say, "You are my God."
My times are in Your hand;
  Deliver me from the hand of my
    enemies,
    And from those who persecute me.

Psalm 31:14–15

For none of us lives to himself, and no
one dies to himself. For if we live, we live
to the Lord; and if we die, we die to the
Lord. Therefore, whether we live or die,
we are the Lord's.

Romans 14:7–8

The days of our lives are seventy years;
    And if by reason of strength they are
        eighty years,
    Yet their boast is only labor and
        sorrow;
    For it is soon cut off, and we fly
        away. . . .
So teach us to number our days,
    That we may gain a heart of
        wisdom. . . .
Oh, satisfy us early with Your mercy,
    That we may rejoice and be glad all
        our days!

Psalm 90:10, 12, 14

"And it shall come to pass afterward
    That I will pour out My Spirit on all
        flesh;
    Your sons and your daughters shall
        prophesy,
    Your old men shall dream dreams,
    Your young men shall see visions."

Joel 2:28

Call on God's Divine Protection

The Lord is my light and my salvation;
 Whom shall I fear?
 The Lord is the strength of my life;
 Of whom shall I be afraid?
When the wicked came against me
 To eat up my flesh,
 My enemies and foes,
 They stumbled and fell.
Though an army may encamp against
   me,
 My heart shall not fear;
 Though war may rise against me,
 In this I will be confident.

Psalm 27:1–3

I will both lie down in peace, and sleep;
  For You alone, O Lord, make me
    dwell in safety.

Psalm 4:8

He who dwells in the secret place of the
    Most High
  Shall abide under the shadow of the
    Almighty.
I will say of the Lord, "He is my refuge
    and my fortress;
  My God, in Him I will trust."

Psalm 91:1–2

The angel of the Lord encamps all
    around those who fear Him,
  And delivers them.

Psalm 34:7

"But whoever listens to me will dwell
    safely,
  And will be secure, without fear
    of evil."

Proverbs 1:33

Be Content with Themselves

"For the mountains shall depart
 And the hills be removed,
 But My kindness shall not depart
 from you,
 Nor shall My covenant of peace be
 removed,"
 Says the Lord, who has mercy
 on you.

Isaiah 54:10

"All your children shall be taught by the
 Lord,
 And great shall be the peace of your
 children."

Isaiah 54:13

Not that I speak in regard to need, for I have learned in whatever state I am, to be content: I know how to be abased, and I know how to abound. Everywhere and in all things I have learned both to be full and to be hungry, both to abound and to suffer need.

Philippians 4:11–12

Now godliness with contentment is great gain. For we brought nothing into this world, and it is certain we can carry nothing out. And having food and clothing, with these we shall be content.

1 Timothy 6:6–8

The LORD will guide you continually,
    And satisfy your soul in drought,
    And strengthen your bones;
    You shall be like a watered garden,
    And like a spring of water, whose
        waters do not fail.

Isaiah 58:11

The Lord is your keeper;
>   The Lord is your shade at your right
>   hand.
The sun shall not strike you by day,
>   Nor the moon by night.
The Lord shall preserve you from all
>   evil;
>   He shall preserve your soul.
The Lord shall preserve your going out
>   and your coming in
>   From this time forth, and even
>   forevermore.

Psalm 121:5–8

As it is written:
>   "Eye has not seen, nor ear heard,
>   Nor have entered into the heart of
>   man
>   The things which God has prepared
>   for those who love Him."

1 Corinthians 2:9

God Teaches
Mothers
How to . . .

GOD TEACHES MOTHERS HOW TO . . .

Trust Him Completely

The LORD is my shepherd;
    I shall not want.
He makes me to lie down in green
        pastures;
    He leads me beside the still waters.
He restores my soul;
    He leads me in the paths of
        righteousness
    For His name's sake.
Yea, though I walk through the valley of
        the shadow of death,
    I will fear no evil;
    For You are with me;
    Your rod and Your staff, they
        comfort me.

Psalm 23:1–4

I will say of the LORD, "He is my refuge
and my fortress;
My God, in Him I will trust."
Surely He shall deliver you from the
snare of the fowler
And from the perilous pestilence.
He shall cover you with His feathers,
And under His wings you shall take
refuge;
His truth shall be your shield and
buckler.

Psalm 91:2–4

But know that the LORD has set apart for
Himself him who is godly;
The LORD will hear when I call to
Him. . . .
Offer the sacrifices of righteousness,
And put your trust in the LORD.

Psalm 4:3, 5

Trust in the Lord with all your heart,
And lean not on your own
understanding;
In all your ways acknowledge Him,
And He shall direct your paths.

Proverbs 3:5–6

Trust in the Lord, and do good;
Dwell in the land, and feed on His
faithfulness.
Delight yourself also in the Lord,
And He shall give you the desires of
your heart.
Commit your way to the Lord,
Trust also in Him,
And He shall bring it to pass.

Psalm 37:3–5

Every word of God is pure;
He is a shield to those who put their
trust in Him.

Proverbs 30:5

Hold On to Faith

Let us hold fast the confession of our hope without wavering, for He who promised is faithful.

Hebrews 10:23

Stand therefore . . . having shod your feet with the preparation of the gospel of peace; above all, taking the shield of faith with which you will be able to quench all the fiery darts of the wicked one.

Ephesians 6:14–16

But you, beloved, building yourselves up on your most holy faith, praying in the Holy Spirit, keep yourselves in the love of God, looking for the mercy of our Lord Jesus Christ unto eternal life.

Jude vv. 20–21

"Have I not commanded you? Be strong and of good courage; do not be afraid, nor be dismayed, for the LORD your God is with you wherever you go."

Joshua 1:9

So then faith comes by hearing, and hearing by the word of God.

Romans 10:17

So Jesus said to them, "Because of your unbelief; for assuredly, I say to you, if you have faith as a mustard seed, you will say to this mountain, 'Move from here to there,' and it will move; and nothing will be impossible for you. However, this kind does not go out except by prayer and fasting."

Matthew 17:20–21

For we walk by faith, not by sight.

2 Corinthians 5:7

Have Joy in Him

"If you keep My commandments, you will abide in My love, just as I have kept My Father's commandments and abide in His love.

"These things I have spoken to you, that My joy may remain in you, and that your joy may be full."

John 15:10–11

Let us come before His presence with
      thanksgiving;
  Let us shout joyfully to Him with
      psalms.

Psalm 95:2

Yet I will rejoice in the LORD,
  I will joy in the God of my salvation.

Habakkuk 3:18

Because Your lovingkindness is better
     than life,
    My lips shall praise You.
Thus I will bless You while I live;
    I will lift up my hands in Your
     name.
My soul shall be satisfied as with
     marrow and fatness,
    And my mouth shall praise You
     with joyful lips.

Psalm 63:3–5

Oh, send out Your light and Your truth!
    Let them lead me;
    Let them bring me to Your holy hill
    And to Your tabernacle.
Then I will go to the altar of God,
    To God my exceeding joy;
    And on the harp I will praise You,
    O God, my God.

Psalm 43:3–4

Rest in His Protection

"No weapon formed against you shall
        prosper,
    And every tongue which rises
        against you in judgment
    You shall condemn.
    This is the heritage of the servants
        of the LORD,
    And their righteousness is from Me,"
    Says the LORD.

Isaiah 54:17

Thus says the LORD:
    "Stand in the ways and see,
    And ask for the old paths, where the
        good way is,
    And walk in it;
    Then you will find rest for your
        souls."

Jeremiah 6:16

The Lord is my light and my salvation;
  Whom shall I fear?
  The Lord is the strength of my life;
  Of whom shall I be afraid?
When the wicked came against me
  To eat up my flesh,
  My enemies and foes,
  They stumbled and fell.
Though an army may encamp
      against me,
  My heart shall not fear;
  Though war may rise against me,
  In this I will be confident.
One thing I have desired of the Lord,
  That will I seek:
  That I may dwell in the house of the
      Lord
  All the days of my life,
  To behold the beauty of the Lord,
  And to inquire in His temple.
For in the time of trouble
  He shall hide me in His pavilion;
  In the secret place of His tabernacle
  He shall hide me;
  He shall set me high upon a rock.

Psalm 27:1–5

I cry out to the LORD with my voice;
  With my voice to the LORD I make
    my supplication.
I pour out my complaint before Him;
  I declare before Him my trouble.

Psalm 142:1–2

Rest in the LORD, and wait patiently for
    Him;
  Do not fret because of him who
    prospers in his way,
  Because of the man who brings
    wicked schemes to pass.
Cease from anger, and forsake wrath;
  Do not fret—it only causes
    harm. . . .
But the meek shall inherit the earth,
  And shall delight themselves in the
    abundance of peace.

Psalm 37:7–8, 11

Obtain His Promise

"But seek first the kingdom of God and His righteousness, and all these things shall be added to you."

Matthew 6:33

And we desire that each one of you show the same diligence to the full assurance of hope until the end, that you do not become sluggish, but imitate those who through faith and patience inherit the promises.

Hebrews 6:11–12

And the angel answered . . . "For with God nothing will be impossible."

Luke 1:35, 37

[There] have been given to us exceedingly great and precious promises, that through these you may be partakers of the divine nature, having escaped the corruption that is in the world through lust.

But also for this very reason, giving all diligence, add to your faith virtue, to virtue knowledge, to knowledge self-control, to self-control perseverance, to perseverance godliness, to godliness brotherly kindness, and to brotherly kindness love. For if these things are yours and abound, you will be neither barren nor unfruitful in the knowledge of our Lord Jesus Christ.

2 Peter 1:4–8

He did not waver at the promise of God through unbelief, but was strengthened in faith, giving glory to God, and being fully convinced that what He had promised He was also able to perform.

Romans 4:20–21

Praise His Might

Praise the LORD!
> Praise the LORD, O my soul!

While I live I will praise the LORD;
> I will sing praises to my God while I
> have my being.

Psalm 146:1–2

Praise the LORD!
> Oh, give thanks to the LORD, for He
> is good!

For His mercy endures forever.
Who can utter the mighty acts of the
> LORD?
> Who can declare all His praise?

Psalm 106:1–2

Praise the LORD!
>Praise the LORD from the heavens;
>Praise Him in the heights!
Praise Him, all His angels;
>Praise Him, all His hosts!
Praise Him, sun and moon;
>Praise Him, all you stars of light!
Praise Him, you heavens of heavens,
>And you waters above the heavens!
Let them praise the name of the LORD,
>For He commanded and they were
>created.

Psalm 148:1–5

Praise the LORD!
>Praise, O servants of the LORD,
>Praise the name of the LORD!
Blessed be the name of the LORD
>From this time forth and
>forevermore!
From the rising of the sun to its
>going down
>The LORD's name is to be praised.

Psalm 113:1–3

Praise the LORD!
    Praise God in His sanctuary;
    Praise Him in His mighty
        firmament!
Praise Him for His mighty acts;
    Praise Him according to His
        excellent greatness!
Praise Him with the sound of the
        trumpet;
    Praise Him with the lute and harp!
Praise Him with the timbrel and dance;
    Praise Him with stringed
        instruments and flutes!
Praise Him with loud cymbals;
    Praise Him with clashing cymbals!
Let everything that has breath
        praise the LORD.
    Praise the LORD!

Psalm 150:1–6

Trust in His Power

You will keep him in perfect peace,
　　Whose mind is stayed on You,
　　Because he trusts in You.
Trust in the LORD forever,
　　For in YAH, the LORD, is everlasting
　　　　strength.

Isaiah 26:3–4

But the salvation of the righteous is
　　　　from the LORD;
　　He is their strength in the time of
　　　　trouble.
And the LORD shall help them and
　　　　deliver them;
　　He shall deliver them from the
　　　　wicked,
　　And save them,
　　Because they trust in Him.

Psalm 37:39–40

The LORD is on my side;
    I will not fear.
    What can man do to me? . . .
It is better to trust in the LORD
    Than to put confidence in man.

Psalm 118:6, 8

For You are my hope, O Lord GOD;
    You are my trust from my youth. . . .
Let my mouth be filled with Your praise
    And with Your glory all the day.

Psalm 71:5, 8

Blessed be the God and Father of our Lord Jesus Christ, who according to His abundant mercy has begotten us again to a living hope through the resurrection of Jesus Christ from the dead, to an inheritance incorruptible and undefiled and that does not fade away, reserved in heaven for you, who are kept by the power of God through faith for salvation ready to be revealed in the last time.

1 Peter 1:3–5

Now may the God of hope fill you with all joy and peace in believing, that you may abound in hope by the power of the Holy Spirit.

Romans 15:13

For I am not ashamed of the gospel of Christ, for it is the power of God to salvation for everyone who believes, for the Jew first and also for the Greek. For in it the righteousness of God is revealed from faith to faith; as it is written, "The just shall live by faith."

Romans 1:16–17

Pray for His Will

Be anxious for nothing, but in everything by prayer and supplication, with thanksgiving, let your requests be made known to God; and the peace of God, which surpasses all understanding, will guard your hearts and minds through Christ Jesus.

Philippians 4:6–7

Therefore do not be unwise, but understand what the will of the Lord is. And do not be drunk with wine, in which is dissipation; but be filled with the Spirit, speaking to one another in psalms and hymns and spiritual songs, singing and making melody in your heart to the Lord.

Ephesians 5:17–19

Now this is the confidence that we have in Him, that if we ask anything according to His will, He hears us. And if we know that He hears us, whatever we ask, we know that we have the petitions that we have asked of Him.

1 John 5:14–15

But the end of all things is at hand; therefore be serious and watchful in your prayers. And above all things have fervent love for one another, for "love will cover a multitude of sins." Be hospitable to one another without grumbling. As each one has received a gift, minister it to one another, as good stewards of the manifold grace of God.

1 Peter 4:7–10

As for me, I will call upon God,
    And the LORD shall save me.
Evening and morning and at noon
    I will pray, and cry aloud,
    And He shall hear my voice.

Psalm 55:16–17

"For I have come down from heaven, not to do My own will, but the will of Him who sent Me. This is the will of the Father who sent Me, that of all He has given Me I should lose nothing, but should raise it up at the last day. And this is the will of Him who sent Me, that everyone who sees the Son and believes in Him may have everlasting life; and I will raise him up at the last day."

John 6:38–40

For this reason we also, since the day we heard it, do not cease to pray for you, and to ask that you may be filled with the knowledge of His will in all wisdom and spiritual understanding; that you may walk worthy of the Lord, fully pleasing Him, being fruitful in every good work and increasing in the knowledge of God.

Colossians 1:9–10

Rejoice in His Presence

"This Book of the Law shall not depart from your mouth, but you shall meditate in it day and night, that you may observe to do according to all that is written in it. For then you will make your way prosperous, and then you will have good success."

Joshua 1:8

The Lord will command His
     lovingkindness in the daytime,
And in the night His song shall be
     with me—
A prayer to the God of my life.

Psalm 42:8

The law of the LORD is perfect,
    converting the soul;
    The testimony of the LORD is sure,
      making wise the simple.

Psalm 19:7

I will greatly rejoice in the LORD,
    My soul shall be joyful in my God;
    For He has clothed me with the
      garments of salvation,
    He has covered me with the robe of
      righteousness,
    As a bridegroom decks himself with
      ornaments,
    And as a bride adorns herself with
      her jewels.
For as the earth brings forth its bud,
    As the garden causes the things that
      are sown in it to spring forth,
    So the Lord GOD will cause
      righteousness and praise to
      spring forth before all the
      nations.

Isaiah 61:10–11

Live God-Centered Lives

Do not love the world or the things in the world. If anyone loves the world, the love of the Father is not in him. For all that is in the world—the lust of the flesh, the lust of the eyes, and the pride of life—is not of the Father but is of the world. And the world is passing away, and the lust of it; but he who does the will of God abides forever.

1 John 2:15–17

Denying ungodliness and worldly lusts, we should live soberly, righteously, and godly in the present age, looking for the blessed hope and glorious appearing of our great God and Savior Jesus Christ.

Titus 2:12–13

I have been crucified with Christ; it is no longer I who live, but Christ lives in me; and the life which I now live in the flesh I live by faith in the Son of God, who loved me and gave Himself for me.

Galatians 2:20

There is therefore now no condemnation to those who are in Christ Jesus, who do not walk according to the flesh, but according to the Spirit. For the law of the Spirit of life in Christ Jesus has made me free from the law of sin and death.

Romans 8:1–2

Let the word of Christ dwell in you richly in all wisdom, teaching and admonishing one another in psalms and hymns and spiritual songs, singing with grace in your hearts to the Lord.

Colossians 3:16

Cope with Change

Now this I say lest anyone should deceive you with persuasive words. For though I am absent in the flesh, yet I am with you in spirit, rejoicing to see your good order and the steadfastness of your faith in Christ.

As you therefore have received Christ Jesus the Lord, so walk in Him, rooted and built up in Him and established in the faith, as you have been taught, abounding in it with thanksgiving.

Colossians 2:4–7

Trust in the LORD with all your heart,
    And lean not on your own
        understanding;
In all your ways acknowledge Him,
    And He shall direct your paths.

Proverbs 3:5–6

I will bless the LORD who has given
      me counsel;
    My heart also instructs me in the
      night seasons.
I have set the LORD always before me;
    Because He is at my right hand I
      shall not be moved.
Therefore my heart is glad, and my glory
      rejoices;
    My flesh also will rest in hope. . . .
You will show me the path of life;
    In Your presence is fullness of joy;
    At Your right hand are pleasures
      forevermore.

Psalm 16:7–9, 11

For I know the thoughts that I think
toward you, says the LORD, thoughts of
peace and not of evil, to give you a future
and a hope. Then you will call upon Me
and go and pray to Me, and I will listen
to you. And you will seek Me and find
Me, when you search for Me with all
your heart.

Jeremiah 29:11–13

God Walks

with

Mothers . . .

Through Heartache

"The LORD will guide you continually,
   And satisfy your soul in drought,
   And strengthen your bones;
   You shall be like a watered garden,
   And like a spring of water, whose
      waters do not fail."

Isaiah 58:11

The LORD is near to those who have a
      broken heart,
   And saves such as have a contrite
      spirit.
Many are the afflictions of the
      righteous,
   But the LORD delivers him out of
      them all.

Psalm 34:18–19

With my whole heart I have sought You;
  Oh, let me not wander from Your
    commandments!
Your word I have hidden in my heart,
  That I might not sin against You.
Blessed are You, O Lord!
  Teach me Your statutes.
With my lips I have declared
  All the judgments of Your mouth.
I have rejoiced in the way of Your
    testimonies,
  As much as in all riches.
I will meditate on Your precepts,
  And contemplate Your ways.
I will delight myself in Your statutes;
  I will not forget Your word.

Psalm 119:10–16

He who trusts in his own heart is a fool,
  But whoever walks wisely will be
    delivered.

Proverbs 28:26

Through Adversity

Beloved, do not think it strange concerning the fiery trial which is to try you, as though some strange thing happened to you; but rejoice to the extent that you partake of Christ's sufferings, that when His glory is revealed, you may also be glad with exceeding joy.

1 Peter 4:12–13

The LORD will perfect that which
concerns me;
Your mercy, O LORD, endures forever;
Do not forsake the works of Your
hands.

Psalm 138:8

The fear of man brings a snare,
But whoever trusts in the LORD shall
be safe.

Proverbs 29:25

And He said to me, "My grace is sufficient for you, for My strength is made perfect in weakness." Therefore most gladly I will rather boast in my infirmities, that the power of Christ may rest upon me.

2 Corinthians 12:9

The LORD will give strength to His
     people;
     The LORD will bless His people with
          peace.

Psalm 29:11

Finally, my brethren, be strong in the Lord and in the power of His might. Put on the whole armor of God, that you may be able to stand against the wiles of the devil. . . . Therefore take up the whole armor of God, that you may be able to withstand in the evil day, and having done all, to stand.

Ephesians 6:10–11, 13

Through Danger

My soul, wait silently for God alone,
   For my expectation is from Him.
He only is my rock and my salvation;
   He is my defense;
   I shall not be moved.
In God is my salvation and my glory;
   The rock of my strength,
   And my refuge, is in God.

Psalm 62:5–7

"When you pass through the waters, I
      will be with you;
   And through the rivers, they shall
      not overflow you.
   When you walk through the fire,
      you shall not be burned,
   Nor shall the flame scorch you."

Isaiah 43:2

You number my wanderings;
    Put my tears into Your bottle;
    Are they not in Your book?
When I cry out to You,
    Then my enemies will turn back;
    This I know, because God is for me.
In God (I will praise His word),
    In the Lord (I will praise His word),
In God I have put my trust;
    I will not be afraid.
    What can man do to me?

Psalm 56:8–11

He raises the poor out of the dust,
    And lifts the needy out of the ash
        heap. . . .
He grants the barren woman a home,
    Like a joyful mother of children.
    Praise the Lord!

Psalm 113:7, 9

How precious is Your lovingkindness,
O God!
Therefore the children of men put
their trust under the shadow of
Your wings.

Psalm 36:7

Hear my cry, O God;
Attend to my prayer.
From the end of the earth I will cry to
You,
When my heart is overwhelmed;
Lead me to the rock that is higher
than I.
For You have been a shelter for me,
A strong tower from the enemy.
I will abide in Your tabernacle forever;
I will trust in the shelter of Your
wings.

Psalm 61:1–4

Through Impatience

Therefore be patient, brethren, until the coming of the Lord. See how the farmer waits for the precious fruit of the earth, waiting patiently for it until it receives the early and latter rain. You also be patient. Establish your hearts, for the coming of the Lord is at hand.

James 5:7–8

Wait on the LORD;
    Be of good courage,
    And He shall strengthen your heart;
    Wait, I say, on the LORD!

Psalm 27:14

Now we exhort you, brethren, warn those who are unruly, comfort the faint-hearted, uphold the weak, be patient with all. See that no one renders evil for evil to anyone, but always pursue what is good both for yourselves and for all.

1 Thessalonians 5:14–15

For whatever things were written before were written for our learning, that we through the patience and comfort of the Scriptures might have hope. Now may the God of patience and comfort grant you to be like-minded toward one another, according to Christ Jesus, that you may with one mind and one mouth glorify the God and Father of our Lord Jesus Christ.

Romans 15:4–6

But, beloved, we are confident of better things concerning you, yes, things that accompany salvation, though we speak in this manner. For God is not unjust to forget your work and labor of love which you have shown toward His name, in that you have ministered to the saints, and do minister. And we desire that each one of you show the same diligence to the full assurance of hope until the end, that you do not become sluggish, but imitate those who through faith and patience inherit the promises.

Hebrews 6:9–12

My brethren, count it all joy when you fall into various trials, knowing that the testing of your faith produces patience. But let patience have its perfect work, that you may be perfect and complete, lacking nothing.

James 1:2–4

Through Disappointment

LORD, I cry out to You;
    Make haste to me!
    Give ear to my voice when I cry out
      to You.
Let my prayer be set before You as
      incense,
    The lifting up of my hands as the
      evening sacrifice.

Psalm 141:1–2

Now godliness with contentment is great gain. For we brought nothing into this world, and it is certain we can carry nothing out. And having food and clothing, with these we shall be content.

1 Timothy 6:6–8

I have fought the good fight, I have finished the race, I have kept the faith. Finally, there is laid up for me the crown of righteousness, which the Lord, the righteous Judge, will give to me on that Day, and not to me only but also to all who have loved His appearing.

2 Timothy 4:7–8

For I want you to know what a great conflict I have for you and those in Laodicea, and for as many as have not seen my face in the flesh, that their hearts may be encouraged, being knit together in love, and attaining to all riches of the full assurance of understanding, to the knowledge of the mystery of God, both of the Father and of Christ, in whom are hidden all the treasures of wisdom and knowledge.

Colossians 2:1–3

Through Failure

Cast your burden on the LORD,
    And He shall sustain you;
    He shall never permit the righteous
        to be moved.

Psalm 55:22

He has not dealt with us according to
        our sins,
    Nor punished us according to our
        iniquities.
For as the heavens are high above
        the earth,
    So great is His mercy toward those
        who fear Him;
As far as the east is from the west,
    So far has He removed our
        transgressions from us.

Psalm 103:10–12

Now may our Lord Jesus Christ Himself, and our God and Father, who has loved us and given us everlasting consolation and good hope by grace, comfort your hearts and establish you in every good word and work.

2 Thessalonians 2:16–17

[Love] bears all things, believes all things, hopes all things, endures all things.

1 Corinthians 13:7

The LORD gave them rest all around, according to all that He had sworn to their fathers. And not a man of all their enemies stood against them; the LORD delivered all their enemies into their hand. Not a word failed of any good thing which the LORD had spoken to the house of Israel. All came to pass.

Joshua 21:44–45

Has His mercy ceased forever?
Has His promise failed forevermore?
Has God forgotten to be gracious?
Has He in anger shut up His tender
mercies?
And I said, "This is my anguish;
But I will remember the years of the
right hand of the Most High."
I will remember the works of the Lord;
Surely I will remember Your
wonders of old.
I will also meditate on all Your work,
And talk of Your deeds.
Your way, O God, is in the sanctuary;
Who is so great a God as our God?

Psalm 77:8–13

God Gives
Freely to
Mothers . . .

Hope for Eternal Life

And we know that the Son of God has
come and has given us an understanding, that we may know Him who is true;
and we are in Him who is true, in His
Son Jesus Christ. This is the true God
and eternal life.

1 John 5:20

But God, who is rich in mercy, because
of His great love with which He loved us,
even when we were dead in trespasses,
made us alive together with Christ (by
grace you have been saved), and raised
us up together, and made us sit together
in the heavenly places in Christ Jesus,
that in the ages to come He might show
the exceeding riches of His grace in His
kindness toward us in Christ Jesus.

Ephesians 2:4–7

For the wages of sin is death, but the gift of God is eternal life in Christ Jesus our Lord.

Romans 6:23

For as many as are led by the Spirit of God, these are sons of God. For you did not receive the spirit of bondage again to fear, but you received the Spirit of adoption by whom we cry out, "Abba, Father." The Spirit Himself bears witness with our spirit that we are children of God, and if children, then heirs—heirs of God and joint heirs with Christ, if indeed we suffer with Him, that we may also be glorified together.

For I consider that the sufferings of this present time are not worthy to be compared with the glory which shall be revealed in us.

Romans 8:14–18

Wisdom for Daily Living

But the wisdom that is from above is first pure, then peaceable, gentle, willing to yield, full of mercy and good fruits, without partiality and without hypocrisy.

James 3:17

The fear of the LORD is the beginning of
wisdom;
A good understanding have all those
who do His commandments.
His praise endures forever.

Psalm 111:10

How much better to get wisdom than
gold!
And to get understanding is to be
chosen rather than silver.

Proverbs 16:16

For the Lord gives wisdom;
   From His mouth come knowledge
      and understanding;
He stores up sound wisdom for the
         upright;
   He is a shield to those who walk
      uprightly;
He guards the paths of justice,
   And preserves the way of His saints.
Then you will understand righteousness
      and justice,
   Equity and every good path.
When wisdom enters your heart,
   And knowledge is pleasant to your soul,
Discretion will preserve you;
   Understanding will keep you.

Proverbs 2:6–11

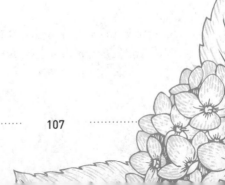

Victory over Sin

Stand fast therefore in the liberty by which Christ has made us free, and do not be entangled again with a yoke of bondage.

Galatians 5:1

And you know that He was manifested to take away our sins, and in Him there is no sin. Whoever abides in Him does not sin. Whoever sins has neither seen Him nor known Him.

Little children, let no one deceive you. He who practices righteousness is righteous, just as He is righteous.

1 John 3:5–7

Create in me a clean heart, O God,
And renew a steadfast spirit
within me.

Psalm 51:10

So when this corruptible has put on incorruption, and this mortal has put on immortality, then shall be brought to pass the saying that is written: "Death is swallowed up in victory."

"O Death, where is your sting?

O Hades, where is your victory?"

The sting of death is sin, and the strength of sin is the law. But thanks be to God, who gives us the victory through our Lord Jesus Christ.

1 Corinthians 15:54–57

For whatever is born of God overcomes the world. And this is the victory that has overcome the world—our faith. Who is he who overcomes the world, but he who believes that Jesus is the Son of God?

1 John 5:4–5

Comfort in Troubled Times

[Cast] all your care upon Him, for He cares for you.

Be sober, be vigilant; because your adversary the devil walks about like a roaring lion, seeking whom he may devour. Resist him, steadfast in the faith, knowing that the same sufferings are experienced by your brotherhood in the world. But may the God of all grace, who called us to His eternal glory by Christ Jesus, after you have suffered a while, perfect, establish, strengthen, and settle you. To Him be the glory and the dominion forever and ever. Amen.

1 Peter 5:7–11

Blessed be the God and Father of our Lord Jesus Christ, the Father of mercies and God of all comfort, who comforts us in all our tribulation, that we may be able to comfort those who are in any trouble, with the comfort with which we ourselves are comforted by God.

2 Corinthians 1:3–4

For thus says the LORD:
> "Behold, I will extend peace to her
>> like a river,
> And the glory of the Gentiles like a
>> flowing stream.
> Then you shall feed;
> On her sides shall you be carried,
> And be dandled on her knees.

As one whom his mother comforts,
> So I will comfort you;
> And you shall be comforted in
>> Jerusalem."

Isaiah 66:12–13

Power to Defeat Fear

Then Jesus spoke to them again, saying, "I am the light of the world. He who follows Me shall not walk in darkness, but have the light of life."

John 8:12

"Fear not, for I am with you;
 Be not dismayed, for I am your God.
 I will strengthen you,
 Yes, I will help you,
 I will uphold you with My righteous
  right hand."

Isaiah 41:10

The fear of the LORD is the beginning of
  knowledge,
 But fools despise wisdom and
  instruction.

Proverbs 1:7

The LORD is my light and my salvation;
  Whom shall I fear?
  The LORD is the strength of my life;
  Of whom shall I be afraid?
When the wicked came against me
  To eat up my flesh,
  My enemies and foes,
  They stumbled and fell.
Though an army may encamp
    against me,
  My heart shall not fear;
  Though war may rise against me,
  In this I will be confident. . . .
And now my head shall be lifted up
    above my enemies all around
    me;
  Therefore I will offer sacrifices of
    joy in His tabernacle;
  I will sing, yes, I will sing praises to
    the LORD.

Psalm 27:1–3, 6

Courage to Be Women of Integrity

The Lord shall judge the peoples;
Judge me, O Lord, according to my
righteousness,
And according to my integrity
within me.

Psalm 7:8

He who walks with integrity walks
securely,
But he who perverts his ways will
become known. . . .
The mouth of the righteous is a well of
life,
But violence covers the mouth of the
wicked.

Proverbs 10:9, 11

If I have walked with falsehood,
    Or if my foot has hastened to deceit,
Let me be weighed on honest scales,
    That God may know my integrity.

Job 31:5–6

Keep my soul, and deliver me;
    Let me not be ashamed, for I put my
        trust in You.
Let integrity and uprightness
        preserve me,
    For I wait for You.

Psalm 25:20–21

When pride comes, then comes shame;
    But with the humble is wisdom.
The integrity of the upright will guide
        them,
    But the perversity of the unfaithful
        will destroy them.

Proverbs 11:2–3

The Peace That Only
He Can Give

"When you pass through the waters, I
   will be with you;
   And through the rivers, they shall
      not overflow you.
   When you walk through the fire,
      you shall not be burned,
   Nor shall the flame scorch you.
For I am the LORD your God,
   The Holy One of Israel, your Savior;
   I gave Egypt for your ransom,
   Ethiopia and Seba in your place.
Since you were precious in My sight,
   You have been honored,
   And I have loved you;
   Therefore I will give men for you,
   And people for your life."

Isaiah 43:2–4

I have called upon You, for You will hear
    me, O God;
    Incline Your ear to me, and hear my
      speech.
Show Your marvelous lovingkindness by
    Your right hand,
    O You who save those who trust in
      You
From those who rise up against them.
    Keep me as the apple of Your eye;
    Hide me under the shadow of Your
      wings.

Psalm 17:6–8

For He Himself is our peace, who has
made both one, and has broken down
the middle wall of separation, having
abolished in His flesh the enmity, that
is, the law of commandments contained
in ordinances, so as to create in Himself
one new man from the two, thus making
peace.

Ephesians 2:14–15

The LORD is high above all nations,
    His glory above the heavens.
Who is like the LORD our God,
    Who dwells on high,
Who humbles Himself to behold
    The things that are in the heavens
        and in the earth?
He raises the poor out of the dust,
    And lifts the needy out of the ash
        heap,
That He may seat him with princes—
    With the princes of His people.
He grants the barren woman a home,
    Like a joyful mother of children.
    Praise the LORD!

Psalm 113:4–9

"Let not your heart be troubled; you believe in God, believe also in Me. In My Father's house are many mansions; if it were not so, I would have told you. I go to prepare a place for you. And if I go and prepare a place for you, I will come again and receive you to Myself; that where I am, there you may be also. And where I go you know, and the way you know. . . .

"Peace I leave with you, My peace I give to you; not as the world gives do I give to you. Let not your heart be troubled, neither let it be afraid. You have heard Me say to you, 'I am going away and coming back to you.' If you loved Me, you would rejoice because I said, 'I am going to the Father,' for My Father is greater than I."

John 14:1–4, 27–28

"Her children rise up and call her blessed."

Proverbs 31:28

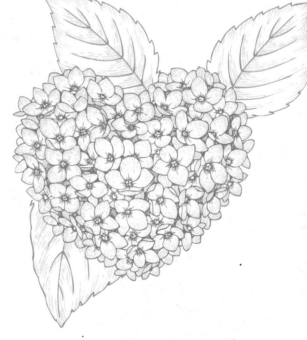

Family Resources Center
415 NE Monroe,
Peoria, IL 61603 (309) 839-2287